SIMPLY CORGIS
THE COLORING BOOK

Part of the Simply Dogs Coloring Book Range

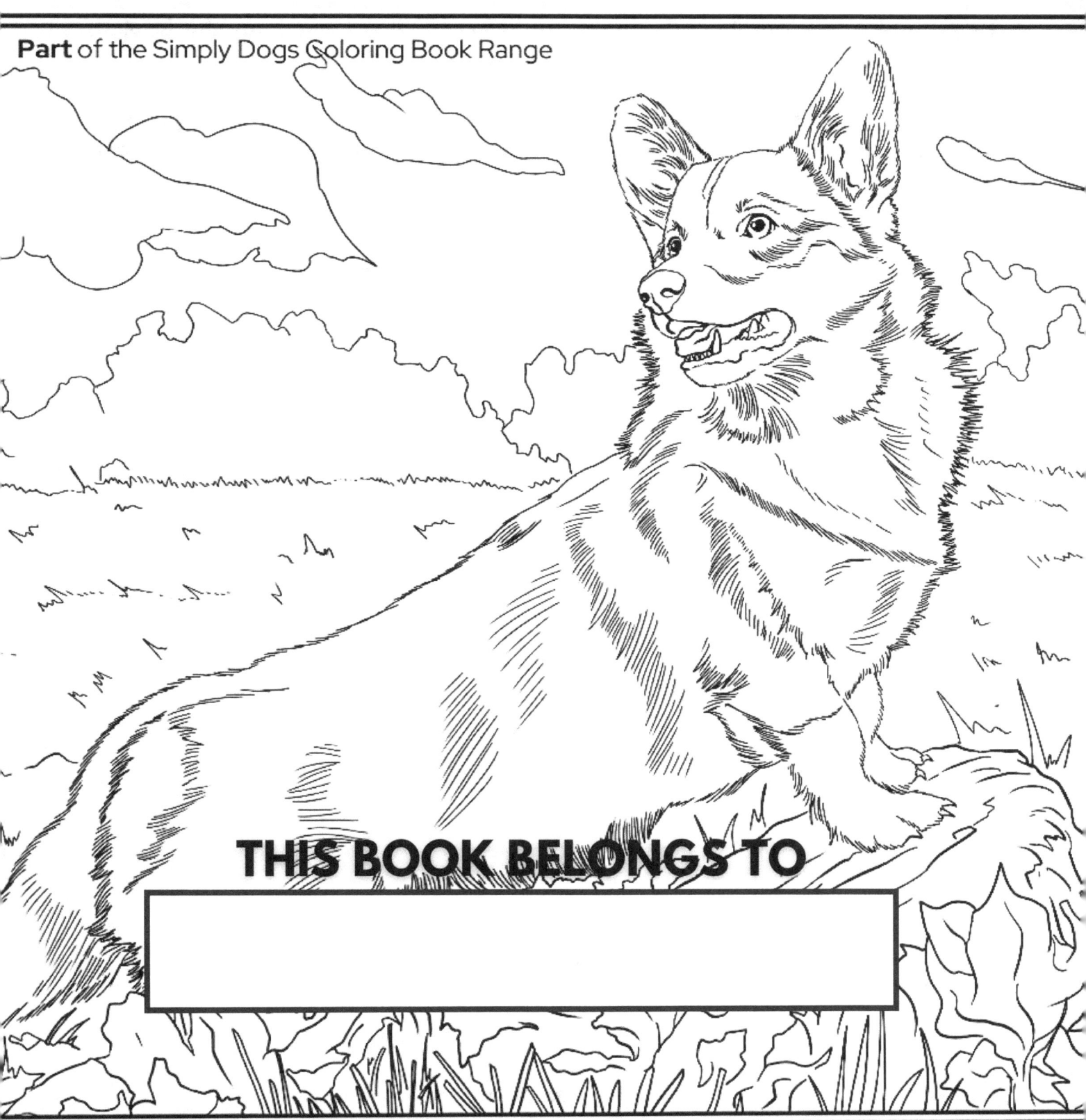

THIS BOOK BELONGS TO

FROM THE PUBLISHER

Hey, thank you for making the purchase, we really hope you enjoy this book. If you have the chance, then all feedback is greatly appreciated.

We have put a lot of effort into making this book, so if you are not completely satisfied, please email us at ben@bclesterbooks.com and we will do our best to address any issues.

If you have any suggestions, enquiries or want to send us a selfie with this book, then email at the same address - ben@bclesterbooks.com

FUNKY FAUCET PRESS

THE CORGI GALLERY
INCLUDING THE FULL RANGE OF COLORING PAGES

READY TO START?

Relax, unwind, and enjoy the experience!

Please note that paint, highlighters and other tools that may cause bleedthrough are NOT recommended with this coloring book.